Let Freedom Ring

Nat Turner

Rebellious Slave

by Susan R. Gregson

Consultant:
Theodore C. DeLaney, Associate Professor of History
Washington and Lee University
Lexington, Virginia

Bridgestone Books
an imprint of Capstone Press
Mankato, Minnesota

Bridgestone Books are published by Capstone Press
151 Good Counsel Drive, P.O. Box 669, Mankato, Minnesota 56002
http://www.capstone-press.com

Printed in the United States of America

Library of Congress Cataloging-in-Publication Data
Gregson, Susan R.
Nat Turner: Rebellious slave/by Susan R. Gregson.
p. cm. — (Let freedom ring)
Summary: A biography of the slave and preacher who, believing that God wanted him to free the slaves, led a major revolt in 1831.
Includes bibliographical references and index.
ISBN 0-7368-1555-4 (hardcover)
1. Turner, Nat, 1800?–1831—Juvenile literature. 2. Southampton Insurrection, 1831—Juvenile literature. 3. Slaves—Virginia—Southampton County—Biography—Juvenile literature. 4. Slave insurrections—Virginia—Southampton County—History—19th century—Juvenile literature. 5. Southampton County (Va.)—History—19th century—Juvenile literature. [1. Turner, Nat, 1800?–1831. 2. Slaves. 3. African Americans—Biography. 4. Southampton Insurrection, 1831.] I. Title. II. Series.
F232.S7 G68 2003
975.5'5503'092—dc21 2002012002

Editorial Credits
Charles Pederson, editor; Kia Adams, series designer; Juliette Peters, book designer; Kelly Garvin, photo researcher; Karen Risch, product planning editor

Photo Credits
Hulton Archive by Getty Images, 10, 19
Library of Congress, cover (small), 5, 38
The Library of Virginia Historical Inventory, 31, 32
North Carolina Office of Archives and History, Raleigh, NC, cover (main), 29
North Wind Picture Archives, 7, 9, 13, 14, 17, 37, 40, 43
PhotoDisc, Inc., 26, 40
Stock Montage, Inc, 21, 23, 25, 42
Virginia Center for Digital History, 39

1 2 3 4 5 6 08 07 06 05 04 03

Table of Contents

Features

Chapter One

Black, White, and Blood-Red

In the early morning of August 22, 1831, seven African American slaves moved quietly through the night. Led by Nat Turner, the men approached a Virginia slave owner's farm home. Inside, the slaves killed the slave owner and his wife and children.

After these killings, the slaves continued their march. They took guns, ammunition, food, liquor, and horses. As the men traveled, they urged other slaves to join them. By dawn, the group had killed more slave owners. The slave rebels then marched to a nearby town's supply of guns and bullets. The slaves planned to start a war to win their freedom.

During a revolt in 1831, Virginia slave rebels used knives and axes to kill their slave owners.

This slave revolt lasted two days. As the group marched and killed, more slaves joined the revolt. Slave owners in the area heard of the violence and came out to fight the slaves. The slave owners severely punished any slaves they caught. The owners beat and even killed some of the slaves.

The slaves' leader, Nat Turner, was a preacher. His followers called him General Nat. Slave owners called him an evil murderer and a madman.

Nat stirs debate even today. Historians and other people agree Nat hoped to strike a blow against slavery. People also agree Nat had the right to rebel against slavery. Slaves sometimes rebelled by running away, pretending to be sick, or breaking tools. Most people agree that the way Nat rebelled, by killing other people, was not right.

Slavery in 1830

In 1830, almost 13 million people lived in the United States. More than 2 million of those people were slaves. In Nat's lifetime, field slaves usually worked at least six days a week from before sunrise until after sunset.

In Nat's time, Southampton County in Virginia had many slave-owning families. The population of the county was about 60 percent African American slaves and 40 percent white. Most slave owners had fewer than 10 slaves. About 15 men owned 15 or more slaves. Three planters in the county owned more than 150 slaves.

Chapter Two

Slavery and Young Nat

A person's life as a slave began in childhood. Young slave children were put to work doing light chores or helping older slaves watch younger children. By the time they reached age 9, many slave children worked in the fields with adult slaves.

Field slaves worked many hours every day. They tended the hot, humid fields, took care of animals, repaired farm buildings, or harvested crops.

Slaves were allowed to eat lunch during a short midday break. At night, the slaves returned to small shacks or cabins with dirt floors and no lights. Before daybreak the next morning, they awoke and headed for the fields once again.

Slave owners usually lived in better conditions than their

Slaves worked in fields from before the sun rose until after it had set.

People as Property

In 1619, the first Africans arrived in North America. John Rolfe, an English tobacco farmer in Jamestown, Virginia, wrote: "About the last of August came [a Dutch ship] that sold us twenty [slaves]."

Slavery increased throughout the American colonies. By the 1770s, about 700,000 slaves lived in the United States. Shortly before U.S. slavery ended in 1865, almost 4 million people were slaves.

When slaves ran away from their farms, their owners sometimes placed ads in local newspapers for the slaves' return. In 1768, the *Virginia Gazette* described one runaway: "Jude . . . has long black hair, a large scar on one of her elbows, and several other scars on her face, and has been subject to running away ever since she was ten years old . . . She is very knowing about house business, can spin, weave, sew, and iron, well . . . Whoever [returns her] to me shall be well rewarded for their trouble."

$1200 TO 1250 DOLLARS! FOR NEGROES!!

THE undersigned wishes to purchase a large lot of NEGROES for the New Orleans market. I will pay $1200 to $1250 for No. 1 young men, and $850 to $1000 for No. 1 young women. In fact I will pay more for likely

NEGROES,

Than any other trader in Kentucky. My office is adjoining the Broadway Hotel, on Broadway, Lexington, Ky., where I or my Agent can always be found.

WM. F. TALBOTT.

LEXINGTON, JULY 2, 1853.

Owners also placed ads to buy or sell slaves. One 1829 poster advertised slaves, rice, books, needles, pins, and other property for sale. The 1853 poster at left is from a slave trader who wanted to buy slaves.

slaves did. Owners with large farms and many slaves had big, comfortable houses. The slaves on these large farms lived in crowded shacks away from the owner's house. On small farms with only a few slaves, owners and slaves sometimes lived together in the same house.

Sometimes slave owners and slaves worked together in the fields. Even though they might do the same work, slaves were forced to work longer hours. Owners often did the easier chores and left the very hard work for the slaves. Slaves received small amounts of food they had to cook themselves. Owners did not pay slaves for their work. Everything slaves had, including their own lives, belonged to the owner.

The law looked at slaves as property rather than people. White slave owners were free to treat slaves as they did their cows, horses, and other farm animals. Slaves could not leave their farm without their owner's permission. Owners could buy or sell slaves at any time and for any reason.

At the time Nat was born, slavery was illegal in most Northern states. Some Northern states did allow slavery as late as 1828. Many slaves tried to run away to Northern states where they could be free. Some slaves successfully escaped, but Southern slave hunters recaptured many who tried. Slave owners beat and sometimes even killed these slaves.

Some slaves living far from Northern states escaped into the swamps or forests near their owners' farms. At night, these escaped slaves sometimes took food from nearby farms. Some slaves in hiding dared to visit family members on neighboring farms.

Nat's Early Life

Nat Turner's parents were slaves on Benjamin Turner's farm. Turner owned a small farm in Southampton County, Virginia. Southampton County was located in the eastern part of Virginia. It shared its southern border with North Carolina.

Nat's mother, Nancy, had not been born a slave. Slave traders had kidnapped her from her home in Africa a few years before Nat's birth. They sold her to work on Turner's farm.

Not much is known about Nat's father, not even his name. He was already a slave on the Turner farm when Nancy arrived there. Before Nat was

Escaping to the Swamp

The Dismal Swamp to the east of Nat's slave home was a dark, wild, and wet place. Some slaves in the area escaped to the swamp and lived there for a while because slave owners had a hard time following and recapturing them. These escaped slaves were sometimes called "maroons." This word comes from the Spanish word "cimarrón," which means "free person." Some people believe that Nat's father escaped to the swamp to live with other maroons.

10 years old, his father ran away and never returned. No one knows for sure why he ran away or whether he escaped to freedom or died trying.

Children of slaves were slaves from the time they were born.

Children of slaves were slaves from birth. Nat was a slave when he was born about 1800. When Nat was a baby, his parents noticed birthmarks on his head and shoulders. Some Africans believed that such birthmarks meant the child was marked for great accomplishments. Nat grew up hearing his family tell him he was born to make important things happen.

Nat the Prophet

Nat was not a typical child. When he was 4 years old, his family claimed he described an event that had occurred before he was born. His family and friends believed he would be a messenger from God. They told him he could see things other people could not. As a result, they called him a prophet.

Nat spoke well and learned to read. He claimed to have learned the alphabet by himself. But most historians believe Nat's owners taught him. The Turners taught Nat to read because they wanted him to be able to read the Christian Bible.

Nat was an eager learner. Besides learning to read, he taught himself to work with clay, paper, gunpowder, and metal. Other slaves looked up to

Nat because of his education and skills. They liked to listen to him tell Bible stories. Nat worked hard in the fields and around the farm. His owner considered him a good slave.

Nat became a religious man. He prayed often because praying comforted him. He also fasted. He believed not eating for a time would cleanse his body and help him become closer to God.

Hearing the Voice

At age 20, as Nat worked and prayed in his owner's field, he thought he heard a voice speak in his head. Nat believed the voice was a spirit like those who spoke to prophets in the Bible. The voice told Nat, "Seek ye the kingdom of heaven and all things shall be added unto you." Nat was not sure what the voice meant. Two years later, Nat heard the voice tell him the same message. Still unsure of what to do, Nat waited for another message.

Nat later said he heard the voice a third time with the same message. He said that he had decided what to do. "I now began to prepare [the other slaves] for my purpose, by telling them something was about to happen."

What Is in a Name?

Slave traders captured Africans and forced them onto ships sailing for America. The slave owners who bought them wanted the slaves to forget about their lives in Africa. They named their slaves William or Mary or gave them other Christian or European names. Some owners named their slaves like pets, calling them Big Boy or Buttercup.

When Benjamin Turner bought Nat's mother, he gave her the English name Nancy. It was common for slaves to take their owner's last name. So, Nat's mother was known as Nancy Turner.

Chapter Three

Prophet and Preacher

In 1810, Benjamin Turner died. His farm and slaves were divided. His son Samuel became Nat's owner.

About this same time, hard economic times hit Virginia. Some slave owners sold their slaves for money. Others hired overseers to make the slaves work harder and faster. Samuel Turner hired a cruel overseer who beat the slaves. To escape the beatings, Nat ran away to a swamp near the farm and was gone for a month. The other slaves were happy because they thought he had escaped to freedom.

Overseers, such as the man at left, made slaves work hard with little rest.

Nat later returned to slavery on Samuel Turner's farm because he heard the spirit's voice. He believed the voice was telling him to stop thinking only of himself. His purpose in life was to help other people. He returned to the farm to begin his work of helping others.

Soon after his return, Nat had a vision of dreamlike images. In his mind, Nat saw the Sun grow dark and drip blood to Earth. He saw white and black human figures fighting with each other. Nat believed he heard a voice. The voice told Nat he would see fighting like this during his life. He must find a way to live through it.

In 1822, Samuel Turner died, and his property was divided and sold. A new slave-owning family, headed by Joseph Travis, bought Nat. By this time, Nat had married a slave woman named Cherry. A farmer who lived near the Travis farm bought Cherry and their children. Slave families were often separated in this way.

Other Slave Revolts

Several slave revolts broke out in and near the United States before Nat's revolt. Some of them may have influenced Nat.

In 1791, slaves on the Caribbean island of Saint Domingue fought against their French owners. Their leader was Toussaint L'Ouverture, shown seated below. In 1804, the former slaves on the island created the country of Haiti. It became the second independent country in the region, after the United States.

Slaves revolted in other places as well. In 1739, the unsuccessful Stono Revolt broke out in South Carolina. In 1800, a Virginia slave named Gabriel Prosser was hanged for planning a revolt. In 1811, slaves near New Orleans were killed in a revolt. In 1822, a free African American named Denmark Vesey was hanged in South Carolina. He and dozens of slaves had planned to take over the city of Charleston. Two of the slaves told their owners about the planned revolt.

More Prayers and Preaching

Still unsure what to do, Nat worked, prayed, and preached to other slaves. He traveled around the countryside on Sundays to preach at neighboring farms. He became a well-known speaker in the area. Nat sometimes even spoke at the churches of slave owners and their families.

As Nat preached at different farms in the area, he came to know the dirt roads that connected the small towns in Southampton County. He learned the way from one slave owner's home to another's. He met many slaves and learned to trust some of them as friends.

In May 1828, Nat again heard the voice in his head. This time, the voice told him to kill his owners with their own weapons. Nat decided he had to use violence to free his people from slavery. He listened for the voice to give him a sign to act.

African American preachers sometimes spoke to slaves and slave owners at the same time. This 1860s illustration shows a worship service similar to one that might have occurred during Nat's time.

Chapter Four

A Call to Arms

Nat waited three years for a sign to act. During those years, he continued to work and preach. He told a few trusted friends about his vision of the fighting human figures. In February 1831, the Moon passed between the Sun and Earth. During this eclipse of the Sun, the Moon's shadow crossed Earth. The sky turned dark during the middle of the day. Nat believed the eclipse was his sign to begin the revolt and free his people from slavery.

Nat gathered four of his closest friends to plan a revolt. During nighttime meetings, Nat told them they must first move through the countryside to kill the white slave owners in Southampton County. They then would travel to the nearby town of Jerusalem and take over weapons stored there.

Nat, leaning on his staff, secretly met with his friends to plan their revolt.

Eclipse of the Sun

A solar eclipse happens when the Moon moves between the Earth and the Sun, blocking the sunlight. Eclipses frightened many people for hundreds of years before Nat's time. People did not know why the sky grew dark in the middle of the day. The darkness sometimes seemed like a sign of bad things to come. Nat believed the solar eclipse he saw was a sign from God to begin his revolt.

Nat and his followers planned to gather more slaves as they marched. He believed they would have an army of slaves by the time they reached Jerusalem.

Planning the Revolt

The slaves planned the revolt for July 4, 1831. On this same date in 1776, the American colonies had declared their independence from Great Britain. Nat may have thought it would be a good day to win the slaves' independence from their owners.

By the time July 4 arrived, Nat canceled the revolt. Nat feared that many slaves would die in the fight. He believed he also might die. He feared that slave owners would hang him if they caught him.

On August 13, 1831, the sky again grew dark because of areas on the sun called sunspots. The sun turned a pale shade of green. Nat believed this occurrence was another sign for the revolt to start. On Sunday, August 21, Nat asked his four followers to meet him in secret.

Nat and his friends ate their evening meal by a fire in the woods. As they ate, they finished their plans for the revolt. His four friends had brought along two other slaves, making a total of seven. The men called Nat "General Nat." They listened as he spoke. He reminded them they were a small group and had to surprise their enemies. They needed to shock the slave owners. They had to act fast, with cruelty. He outlined how they would kill any white people they met.

Nat was sure thousands of slaves would join them. He planned to take over Jerusalem and get more guns and bullets. By the strength of their numbers, Nat and his followers believed they could kill all the slave owners and end slavery. They planned to return to the farms where they had worked as slaves. They then would claim the land.

General Nat Revolts

At first, Nat and his group had only a couple of small axes. They headed to the Travis home. Nat climbed in a window and let his friends in the door. Nat tried to kill his owner, Joseph Travis, with an axe. But Travis managed to escape from Nat.

No More Slave Preachers

Nat's uprising scared many white Southerners. One Virginia newspaper wrote, "The case of Nat Turner warns us. No black man ought to be permitted to turn a Preacher through the country."

After Nat's revolt, Virginia passed laws that made it illegal for slaves to read or write. Other Southern states followed Virginia's lead. They passed their own laws that limited slaves even more. A copy of a law passed in South Carolina on November 30, 1831, appears below. It prevented both slaves and free African Americans from becoming preachers in that state.

A Bill to prevent Slaves or free persons of Colour from preaching within the bounds of this State -

1. Be it enacted by the general assembly of the State of North Carolina and it is hereby enacted by the authority of the same. that from and after the passage of this act it shall not be lawfull for any sect or denomination of religion in this State. to ordain License or Set apart to the Ministry any Slave. or free person of colour.

2. Be it further enacted that no slave or free person of colour from any of the States. or any part of the Globe shall have the privilege of officiating as a Preacher of the Gospel whilst withing the jurisdiction of this State: under penalty of receiving thirty nine lashes on the bare back for every such offence; and fine and imprisonment in a free person of colour. at the discretion of the county court

One of the other slaves killed Travis and his wife. The slaves also killed the Travis children. No one was left alive to warn other slave owners. The slaves took guns and bullets from the Travises and traveled to the next farm. They did not burn homes or destroy property. They stole only horses, food, guns, and other things they needed for battle.

The rebels moved from farm to farm. They killed slave owners and their families at the farms of the Whiteheads, the Wallers, and several others. Some slaves joined the revolt. Others refused because they thought the revolt was wrong or were afraid their owners would catch and kill them. By late Monday morning, Nat's group had grown to about 60 men. Most of the slaves were riding stolen horses.

Slave Owners Fight Back

By Tuesday morning, white people who had escaped Nat's men warned other slave owners about the revolt. Members of local military groups called

Nat and his army attacked this home during his revolt.

militias organized themselves against the slaves. Some slave owners set out on their own to find their escaped slaves. Some slaves were caught and jailed. Residents of nearby towns rang their churches' bells

This home near Jerusalem was used as a jail for slaves captured during Nat's revolt.

to warn people to hide from the revolting slaves. Some farming families fought back when the slaves arrived to kill them.

On the road near the farm of James Parker, 18 white men met the slaves. More slave owners arrived in larger groups.

As the number of white slave owners grew, the number of men in Nat's group became smaller. Some of his men ran away, and slave owners caught or killed others. Nat and the rest of his group left the Parker farm and headed along a road toward a bridge over the Nottoway River. Jerusalem was located on the other side of the bridge. At the bridge, Nat saw a group of slave owners waiting to capture him.

General Nat Retreats

Instead of trying to reach Jerusalem, Nat retreated with about 40 men. They met armed slave owners everywhere. The old weapons Nat's men carried were no match against the slave owners' guns and other weapons. Over the next two days, the slave owners chased and caught many of Nat's group. The last fight took place at the farm of Dr. William Blunt. Blunt and several others had armed themselves and surprised Nat's men. Blunt and his men shot back instead of giving up or running away from Nat's group.

Nat decided to hide. He had sent a few followers to gather more slaves, but none of these followers returned. When armed slave owners reached the area, Nat believed his followers had been captured. He thought they had told the slave owners where he was hiding. He may have been right, because slaves often told their owners about planned revolts.

Nat returned to the Travis farm and dug a hole under a pile of fence rails. He hid there for nearly six weeks. Slave owners moved through the countryside. They looked for Nat and punished anyone they thought was helping him.

Nat Turner's Path

Chapter Five

The End of Nat

Slave owners were quick to take their revenge. Within days, more than 3,000 white men from Virginia and nearby states roamed the roads. These men killed about 200 slaves during the coming weeks. They beat many more slaves, even though most of them were not guilty of helping Nat. Slave owners used even more violence than before to terrify their slaves. They wanted slaves to be too afraid ever to revolt again.

While slave owners punished their slaves, Nat continued to hide under his woodpile. He came out at night to find food and water. Most slaves considered Nat a hero and hoped he had escaped to the North. Slave owners feared and hated Nat. They worried he would return to start another revolt.

Slave owners captured Nat

A slave owner captured Nat as he stepped away from his hiding place.

about six weeks after his rebellion began. They jailed him in Jerusalem, where a judge ordered his trial.

Nat Confesses

While waiting for his trial, Nat told his side of the story to Thomas Gray. Gray published Nat's story as *The Confessions of Nat Turner.* Nat said he knew what he was doing. He claimed his actions to free slaves were right.

During his trial, Nat admitted leading the revolt that killed 55 white people. About half of them were children. On November 5, a jury of white men found Nat guilty of leading the slave revolt. The jury sentenced him to death by hanging.

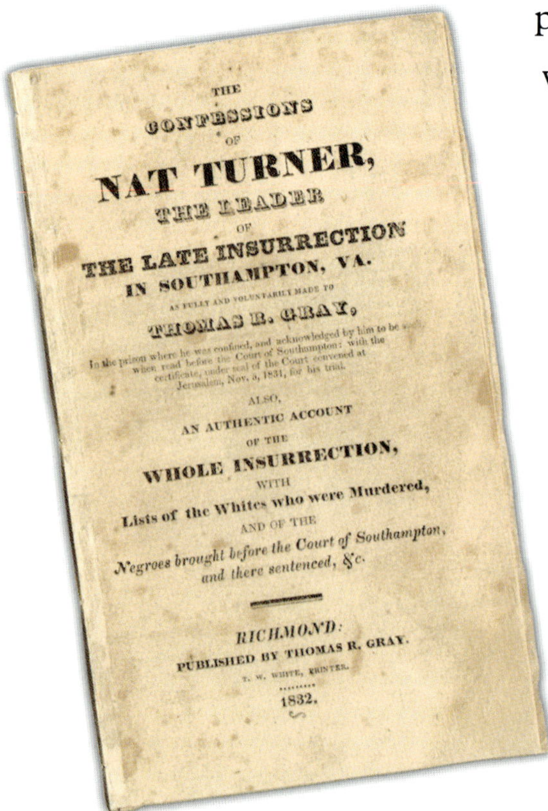

THE

CONFESSIONS

OF

NAT TURNER,

THE LEADER

OF

THE LATE INSURRECTION

IN SOUTHAMPTON, VA.

AS FULLY AND VOLUNTARILY MADE TO

THOMAS R. GRAY,

In the prison where he was confined, and acknowledged by him to be when read before the Court of Southampton; with the certificate, under seal of the Court convened at Jerusalem, Nov. 5, 1831, for his trial.

ALSO,

AN AUTHENTIC ACCOUNT

OF THE

WHOLE INSURRECTION,

WITH

Lists of the Whites who were Murdered,

AND OF THE

Negroes brought before the Court of Southampton, and there sentenced, &c.

RICHMOND:

PUBLISHED BY THOMAS R. GRAY.

T. W. WHITE, PRINTER.

1832.

The lock and key above held Nat in his jail cell before he was hanged.

Abolitionists

Abolitionists were men and women who fought to end slavery. Famous abolitionist Frederick Douglass, right, was 13 years old when Nat Turner was hanged. Like Nat, Douglass was born a slave. Douglass rebelled against slavery by escaping. He left the slave state of Maryland and escaped to New York, where he was a free man. He became a well-known speaker and spent much of his life arguing to end slavery.

In January 1831, Boston's William Lloyd Garrison began publishing an abolitionist newspaper called *The Liberator.* Garrison wrote that he wanted to use every means to end slavery. "On this subject [of slavery], I do not wish to think, or speak, or write in moderation," he wrote.

One of the most famous abolitionists was a writer named Harriet Beecher Stowe. She wrote *Uncle Tom's Cabin,* an antislavery book. It first appeared in 1851 and helped unite the Northern states against slavery. Many people believe it helped begin the Civil War in 1861.

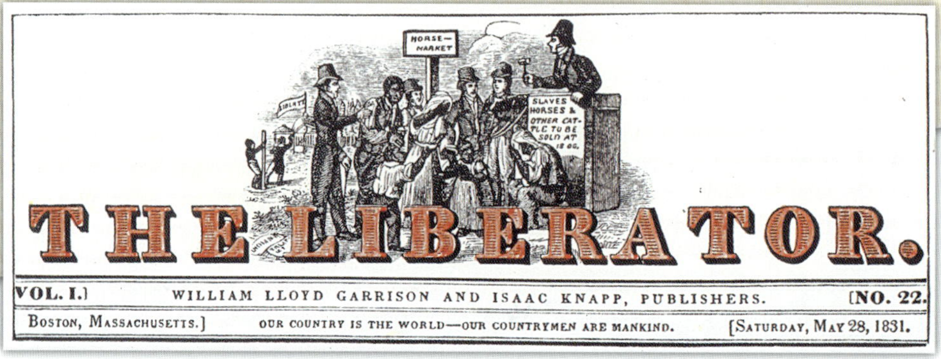

THE LIBERATOR.

VOL. I.] WILLIAM LLOYD GARRISON AND ISAAC KNAPP, PUBLISHERS. [NO. 22.

BOSTON, MASSACHUSETTS.] OUR COUNTRY IS THE WORLD—OUR COUNTRYMEN ARE MANKIND. [SATURDAY, MAY 28, 1831.

On November 11, 1831, a jailer hanged Nat from a tree. A crowd of men, women, and children watched. Viewers of the hanging said Nat died quietly after telling his jailer, "I am ready." No one is certain where Nat was buried.

Severe laws and Nat's death did not end the fight against slavery, which had begun long before Nat was born. Many people continued fighting against slavery until the end of the U.S. Civil War (1861–1865). In late 1865, the 13th Amendment to the U.S. Constitution was passed. It ended slavery in the United States.

In Their Own Words

An article in a Richmond, Virginia, newspaper, named the *Enquirer,* called Nat and his fellow rebels "a parcel of blood-thirsty wolves rushing down from the Alps."

TIMELINE

Chronology of Nat's Life

- 1800: Born on October 2
- 1821: Runs away and later returns to the Turner farm
- 1822: Marries Cherry, another slave

1619 1739 1791 1800 1821 1822

Historical Events

- 1619: The first Africans arrive as slaves in Jamestown, Virginia.
- 1739: Unsuccessful Stono Revolt occurs in South Carolina.
- 1791: Toussaint L'Ouverture's slave revolt begins in Saint Domingue.
- 1800: Gabriel Prosser is put to death for planning a slave revolt.
- 1822: Denmark Vesey's revolt fails.

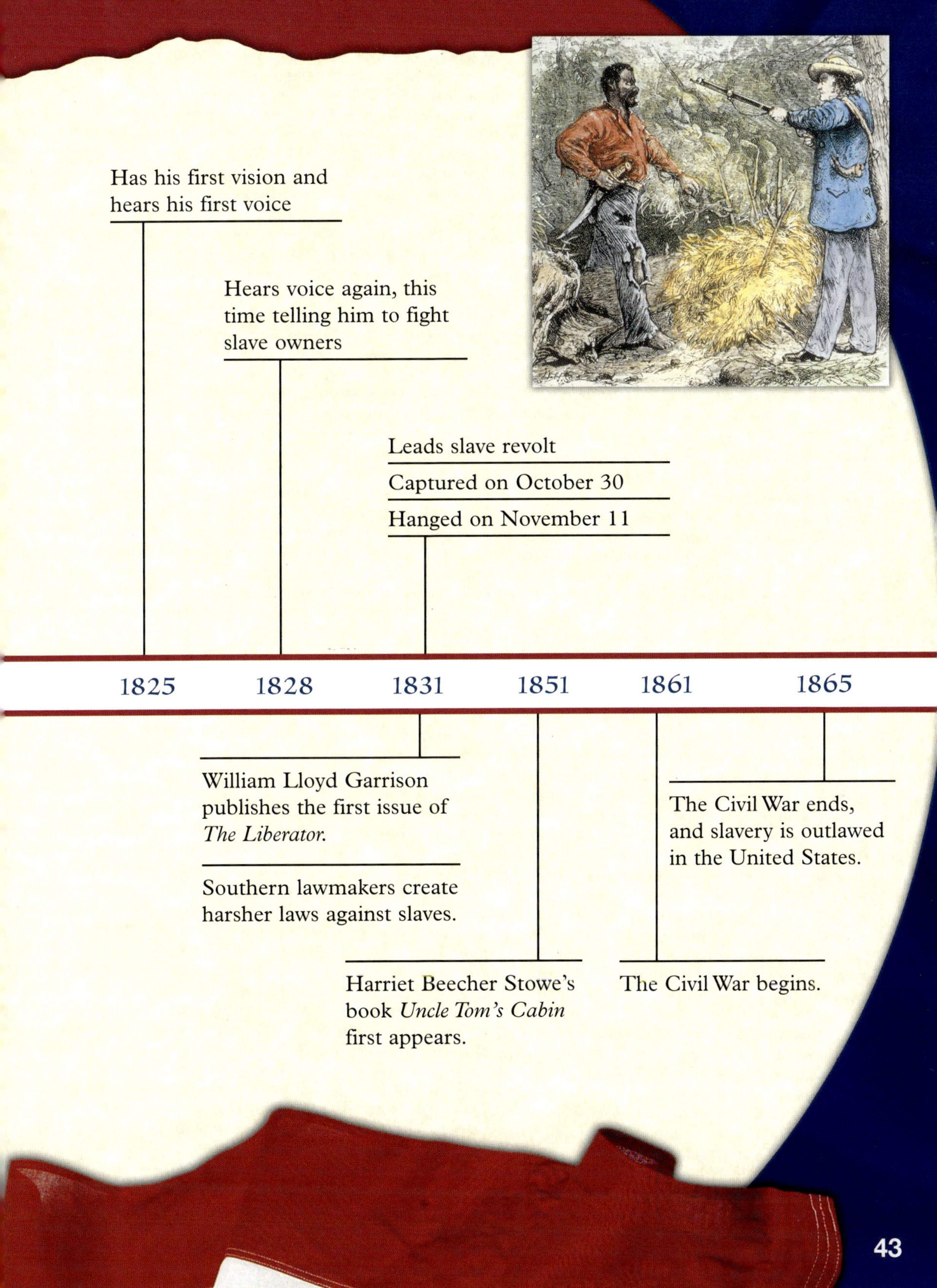

Has his first vision and hears his first voice

Hears voice again, this time telling him to fight slave owners

Leads slave revolt

Captured on October 30

Hanged on November 11

1825	1828	1831	1851	1861	1865

William Lloyd Garrison publishes the first issue of *The Liberator.*

Southern lawmakers create harsher laws against slaves.

Harriet Beecher Stowe's book *Uncle Tom's Cabin* first appears.

The Civil War begins.

The Civil War ends, and slavery is outlawed in the United States.

Glossary

abolitionist (ab-uh-LISH-uh-nist)—a person who fought to end slavery in the United States

fast (FAST)—to go without eating food for a period of time

maroon (muh-ROON)—an escaped slave living in a swamp or forest

militia (muh-LISH-uh)—a group of civilians who form an army during emergencies

overseer (OH-vur-see-ur)—a person hired to make slaves work harder and faster

rebel (REB-uhl)—someone who fights against a government or the people in charge of something

revenge (ri-VENJ)—an action that a person takes to repay harm to someone

revolt (ri-VOHLT)—a fight against a government or an authority

solar eclipse (SOH-lur i-KLIPSS)—a period of daytime darkness when the Moon passes between the Sun and Earth

For Further Reading

Currie, Stephen. *The Liberator: Voice of the Abolitionist Movement.* Words That Changed History. San Diego: Lucent Books, 2000.

De Capua, Sarah. *Abolitionists: A Force for Change.* Journey to Freedom. Chanhassen, Minn.: Child's World, 2002.

Edwards, Judith. *Nat Turner's Slave Rebellion in American History.* In American History. Berkeley Heights, N.J.: Enslow Publishers, 2000.

Isaacs, Sally Senzell. *Life on a Southern Plantation.* Picture the Past. Chicago: Heinemann Library, 2001.

Landau, Elaine. *Slave Narratives: The Journey to Freedom.* In Their Own Voices. New York: Franklin Watts, 2001.

Neshama, Rivvy. *Nat Turner and the Virginia Slave Revolt.* Journey to Freedom. Chanhassen, Minn.: The Child's World, 2001.

Schraff, Anne E. *Frederick Douglass: Speaking Out against Slavery.* African American Biographies. Berkeley Heights, N.J.: Enslow Publishers, 2002.

Places of Interest

African American Civil War Memorial and Museum
1200 U Street, NW
Washington, DC 20009-4443

Eight exhibit areas have displays, including one on slavery and African American leaders such as Nat.

Anacostia Museum and Center for African American History and Culture
1901 Fort Place, SE
Washington, DC 20020

The museum houses exhibits related to African Americans.

Museum of Afro American History
14 Beacon Street
Boston, MA 02108

Exhibits include information on Nat's Southampton revolt.

National Civil Rights Museum
450 Mulberry Street
Memphis, TN 38103-4214

The museum includes information on the civil rights movement and on slavery.

Nat Turner Uprising Site and Trail
Khalifah Health Ranch Retreat
26070 Barhamshill Road
Drewryville, VA 23844-2018

Visitors can see a historical marker and the path Nat took during his revolt.

Internet Sites

Do you want to learn more about Nat Turner?
Visit the FACT HOUND at *http://www.facthound.com*

FACT HOUND can track down many sites to help you. All the FACT HOUND sites are hand-selected by Capstone Press editors. FACT HOUND will fetch the best, most accurate information to answer your questions.

IT IS EASY! IT IS FUN!

1) Go to *http://www.facthound.com*
2) Type in: 0736815554
3) Click on "Fetch It," and FACT HOUND will put you on the trail of several helpful links.

You can also search by subject or book title. So, relax and let our pal FACT HOUND do the research for you!

Index